The Sayings of Jane Austen

G000094554

The Sayings of

JANE
AUSTEN

edited by

Maggie McKernan

Duckworth

Second impression 1997
First published in 1993 by
Gerald Duckworth & Co. Ltd.
The Old Piano Factory
48 Hoxton Square, London N1 6PB
Tel: 071 729 5986
Fax: 071 729 0015

Introduction and editorial arrangement
© 1993 by Maggie McKernan

A catalogue record for this book is available
from the British Library

ISBN 0 7156 2461 X

Typeset by Ray Davies
Printed in Great Britain by
Redwood Press Limited, Trowbridge

Contents

Once, when asked whether he ever read novels, he is said to have replied: 'Oh yes, all six of them every year.'

Dictionary of National Biography

on Gilbert Ryle (d. 1976)

Introduction

'We live at home, quiet, confined, and our feelings prey
upon us.'
                                    Anne Elliot, *Persuasion*

Jane Austen wrote about a world long gone and
regretted – a golden age of leisured gentlemen and
ladies, comfortable, elegant, redolent of a vanished
simplicity and taste. She provides for some an escape
from the bleakness of our time (whenever our time may
be, for her novels have endured many generations of
admirers). She wrote about a world that was insular,
middle-class and deadly.

She was born in 1775, in Steventon in Hampshire, the
second daughter of George Austen, a country
clergyman, cultivated enough to nurture one of the
modern age's most extraordinary talents, and
prosperous enough to provide for the care of seven
children. She was the author of six major novels, *Sense
and Sensibility*, 1811; *Pride and Prejudice*, 1813; *Mansfield
Park*, 1814; *Emma*, 1816; *Northanger Abbey* and *Persuasion*,
1818. She died in 1817. Within her lifetime, she knew a
measure of success, counting among her admirers
Walter Scott and the Prince Regent (to whom *Emma* is
respectfully dedicated upon his own request). She lived
to see four of her major novels in print, the last two
being published one year after her death. And yet, she
was a woman who lived at home, 'quiet, confined', a
doting aunt, a loving sister, her novels written between
the busy little activities of domestic life in the family
parlour. She was born in the Age of Enlightenment,
lived in the age of revolution: the Industrial Revolution,
the American Revolution, the French Revolution. Her
first mature novel *Sense and Sensibility* was begun in
1795, three years after the publication of Wollstonecraft's
Vindication of the Rights of Women. And yet, she wrote
about family life, the '3 or 4 families in a country village'

that formed the basis of her work. She has been called a social satirist, a comedian of manners, the inventor of the modern novel. And yet, her own life is notable only for its lack of events. She wrote about love and marriage. And yet, she herself never married.

'Single women have a dreadful propensity for being poor – which is one strong argument in favour of matrimony' she wrote in a letter to a friend. In this age of new beginnings, poverty, seclusion, ridicule, the fate of an old maid, like Miss Bates in the most perfectly-formed of her novels, *Emma,* was terrible indeed. What work there was for a woman of that class was unenticing – as Miss Bates' poor niece Jane Fairfax had reason to fear: to be a governess, a kind of upper servant, dependent and never at home.

To overlook the absolute and vital necessity of marriage in the world Jane Austen writes about is a fundamental mistake. To see her determined young women as romantic heroines, superior Mills & Boon characters, is an error of the unsophisticated reader. Marriage is simply a cipher for financial and social survival. Wise virgins choose well and look forward to a future of 'perfect happiness'. The foolish, like Maria Bertram in the cautionary *Mansfield Park,* have only the prospect of 'conjugal infelicity', an elegant term that belies the misery of the lovely Mrs Rushworth's brief career.

It's true that the pursuit of a husband, on whom all comfort depended, if a fate like poor Miss Bates', or even poor Miss Austen's, was to be avoided, is the background against which all these small dramas are played out. It's true that they are sweetly innocent of world-shattering events. Yet each of these six novels is deeper and more complex than that implies, and it is upon their many layers of meaning and conjecture, constantly unfolding with each subsequent reading and re-reading, that they lay claim to the highest appreciation.

In *Sense and Sensibility,* the story of two sisters, Elinor and Marianne (an early title for the work), the great matter of love and marriage is all but overshadowed by the nearest thing to evil encountered in the novels. Jane Austen has her rogues, of course, for what is light without darkness, but both Henry Crawford in *Mansfield Park* and Wickham in *Pride and Prejudice* have at least the merit of seducing their peers. Willoughby of *Sense and Sensibility* seduces outside his class – an illegitimate girl, the orphan of a fallen woman – and far from offering her protection he leaves her in wretched and reduced circumstances without hope or help. Even before this is known, Willoughby's character is in doubt. His jilting of Marianne Dashwood, ruthlessly executed, has opened the reader's eyes. 'I could rather believe every creature of my acquaintance leagued together to ruin me in his opinion, than believe his nature capable of such cruelty', cries Marianne. The naked accusation is never made but the words scattered through the novel are used to suggest and convey by a skilful, literary association of ideas – *suspect, design, cruelty, ruin, evil*.

Pride and Prejudice, perhaps the most popular of the six, in welcome contrast, is infused with a certain air of silliness. Perhaps some of its popularity is owed to the fact that almost everyone in it is silly – indeed it contains some of Jane Austen's best comic creations, perhaps the greatest of all of whom is Mr Collins, the superbly stupid clergyman and suitor. 'I flatter myself that … the circumstances of my being next in the entail of Longbourn estate, will be kindly overlooked on your side, and not lead you to reject the offered olive branch', he writes, provoking Elizabeth Bennet to commment: 'We cannot suppose he would help it, if he could.'

Nowhere else do we get such a comprehensive cast of fools. From Mrs Bennet, 'a woman of mean understanding', 'invariably silly', and her husband Mr Bennet, a likeable man but an unpardonably foolish father, their younger daughters, 'two of the silliest girls in the country', to almost all of their acquaintance, like the delightful Sir William Lucas (obsessed with the court of St James – some follies do not date). Jane Bennet, the lesser of the book's pair of heroines, could not be called quick-witted and Elizabeth Bennet herself, delightful and endearing, has inherited so much of her father's wit that she checks herself only with difficulty at the crucial moment of her courtship: 'she remembered that he had yet to learn to be laught at, and it was rather too early to begin.' Twenty-four hours later she is laughing again.

Class, the great winnower, is the major preoccupation of *Emma*. In this novel, whose perfection of symmetry and style reflects the ultimate quest for elegance, everyone has their place, and everybody ultimately stays in it. The 'little bit (two inches wide) of ivory' on which Jane Austen worked had no room on it for upward mobility, despite the efforts of the enterprising climber Mrs Elton (the new bride whose arrival in the village of Highbury threatens to upset the order) and her 'delightful, charming, superior, first circles, spheres, lines, ranks, every thing'. Even Harriet Smith, whom the heroine Emma Woodhouse attempts to raise from respectable illegitimacy to her own level by force of argument ('though in a legal sense she may be called Nobody ... that she is a gentleman's daughter, is indubitable to me; that she associates with gentlemen's daughters, no one, I apprehend, will deny'), marries back into precisely the inferior level she began at. Like Shakespeare's Prospero, Jane Austen's Emma (whom she expected nobody but herself to like) plays with the fates of others and is in the end powerless against fate itself.

If *Sense and Sensibility* has a pervading aura of wickedness, *Mansfield Park* is saturated with virtue. Its heroine, Fanny Price, is not handsome and rich like Emma. The commodity she possesses in abundance is goodness, the sickliness offset by a heartening propensity to point out the faults of others, especially when one of the others is her rival in love, Mary Crawford. Fanny is born good and proves the inefficacy of education in the pursuit of that quality. Transplanted in her early youth to the house of her uncle, she is now in love with her equally upright cousin, Edmund Bertram. When her cousin asks, in one of the moral question and answer sessions they often enjoy, 'Was there nothing in her conversation that struck you Fanny, as not quite right?', she replies without drawing breath: 'Oh! yes, she [Mary Crawford] ought not to have spoken of her uncle as she did. I was quite astonished ... I could not have believed it!' She is gentle, modest and sweet and quite right to doubt Miss Crawford, who turns out to be as flawed as Fanny suspected. Her all-conquering virtue undermines and overturns even Mary's rakish brother Henry. He raises devotion to an almost celestial level: 'You have some touches of the angel in you, beyond what – not merely beyond what one sees, because one never sees any thing like it – but beyond what one fancies might be.' Fanny is 'the perfect model of a woman'.

Catherine Morland is not quite such a perfect heroine. In *Northanger Abbey* there is a great deal of fun and enjoyment. Indeed, the entire novel is a gleeful satire on the prevailing vogue for the Gothic novel. We can well imagine the healthy, normal, 'almost pretty' Catherine Morland, 'rolling down the green slope at the back of the house'. She is enthusiastic in her enjoyments, throws herself into 'a long run of amusement' at Bath, happily anticipates being frightened out of her wits at Northanger Abbey. Her head, like her creator's letters, is full of dancing, clothes and friends. Even Catherine's expulsion from Northanger Abbey, thrown out without an explanation to make her own way home, is an adventure if a little ignominious. All is due to Catherine in return for her unfailing good nature. 'Open, candid, artless, guileless, with affections strong but simple, forming no pretensions, and knowing no disguise.' If *Mansfield Park* is the triumph of virtue, *Northanger Abbey* is the triumph of good nature.

Finally and at last, in *Persuasion*, love itself, unadulterated by expedience or reason, prevails. For this autumnal masterpiece, the tenderest, most moving expressions of the mature emotion are reserved. It was Jane Austen's last completed novel, 'fraught with the apt analogy of the declining year: with declining happiness, and the images of youth and hope, and spring, all gone together.'

As virtuous as Fanny Price, as clever as Emma Woodhouse or Elizabeth Bennet, as feeling as Marianne Dashwood, as good-natured as Catherine Morland, Anne Elliot of *Persuasion* is a reluctant heroine. A single woman, in unenviable circumstances, she faces the prospect of a long and lonely life, blaming no one but herself. It is not marriage that she regrets, but love, and the effect of her loneliness is devastating: 'her attachment and regrets had, for a long time, clouded every enjoyment of youth; and an early loss of bloom and spirits had been their lasting effect.'

Her ultimate reward is a joy only slightly tarnished by the sadness of the lovers' years apart, redeemed by 'all the immortality which the happiest recollections of their own future lives could bestow'.

In the end, we are forced to reacknowledge that, for the heroine of that golden age, that dawn of a new era, marriage was still, after all, the only happy conclusion.

*

Names or words in square brackets indicate the persons or things referred to in the quote. Where dialogue is quoted, the speakers are indicated in brackets in the attribution.

Ladies

Mrs John Dashwood had never been a favourite of her husband's family; but she had had no opportunity, till the present, of shewing them with how little attention to the comfort of other people she could act when occasion required it.

Sense and Sensibility, I.1

Mrs Jennings was a widow, with an ample jointure. She had only two daughters, both of whom she had lived to see respectably married, and she had now therefore nothing to do but to marry all the rest of the world. *Ib.*, I.8

'A woman of seven and twenty,' said Marianne, after pausing a moment,'can never hope to inspire affection again.' *Ib.*

Lady Middleton resigned herself to the idea of it, with all the philosophy of a well bred woman, contenting herself with merely giving her husband a gentle reprimand on the subject five or six times every day. *Ib.*, I.21

Even Lady Middleton took the trouble of being delighted, which was putting herself rather out of her way.

Ib., II.3

Her complexion was sallow; and her features small, without beauty, and naturally without expression; but a lucky contraction of the brow had rescued her countenance from the disgrace of insipidity, by giving it the strong characters of pride and ill nature. [Mrs Ferrars]

Ib., II.12

She was not a woman of many words: for, unlike people in general, she proportioned them to the number of her ideas.

Ib.

'One must allow that there is something very trying to a young woman who *has been* a beauty, in the loss of her personal attractions.'

(Mr John Dashwood), *Ib.*

Her kindness, recommended by so pretty a face, was engaging; her folly, though evident, was not disgusting, because it was not conceited; and Elinor could have forgiven everything but her laugh. [Mrs Palmer]

Ib., III.6

No sooner had he made it clear to himself and his friends that she had hardly a good feature in her face, than he began to find it was rendered uncommonly intelligent by the beautiful expression of her dark eyes. [Elizabeth Bennet]

Pride and Prejudice, I.6

'I have been meditating on the very great pleasure which a pair of fine eyes in the face of a pretty woman can bestow.'

(Mr Darcy), *Ib.*

'A whole day's tête-à-tête between two women can never end without a quarrel.' (Caroline Bingley), *Ib.*, I.7

Jealousy had not yet made her desperate. [Caroline Bingley]

Ib., III.3

'I believe you thought her rather pretty at one time.'
    'Yes,' replied Darcy, who could contain himself no longer,'but *that* was only when I first knew her, for it is many months since I have considered her as one of the handsomest women of my acquaintance.' [Elizabeth Bennet]

(Caroline Bingley & Mr Darcy), *Ib.*, III.3

They could not but hold her cheap on finding that she had but two sashes, and had never learnt French. [Fanny Price]

Mansfield Park, I.2

A young woman, pretty, lively, with a harp as elegant as herself; and both placed near a window, cut down to the ground, and opening on a little lawn, surrounded by shrubs in the rich foliage of summer, was enough to catch any man's heart. [Miss Crawford] *Ib.*, I.7

'A woman can never be too fine while she is all in white.'

(Edmund Bertram), *Ib.*, II.5

'I have always thought her pretty – not strikingly pretty – but "pretty enough" as people say.' [Fanny Price]

(Mary Crawford), *Ib.*, II.6

Although there doubtless are such unconquerable young
ladies of eighteen (or one should not read about them) as
are never to be persuaded into love against their judgement
by all that talent, manner, attention, and flattery can do, I
have no inclination to believe Fanny one of them.   *Ib.*

Miss Crawford, complaisant as a sister, was careless as a
woman and a friend.   *Ib.*, II.8

The gentleness, modesty, and sweetness of her character
were warmly expatiated on, that sweetness which makes so
essential a part of every woman's worth in the judgment of
man, that though he sometimes loves where it is not, he can
never believe it absent. [Mary Crawford]   *Ib.*, II.12

It would not be fair to enquire into a young lady's exact
estimate of her own perfections.   *Ib.*, III.2

'You have some touches of the angel in you, beyond what –
not merely beyond what one sees, because one never sees
any thing like it – but beyond what one fancies might be.'
[Fanny Price]   (Mr Crawford), *Ib.*, III.3

'You have proved yourself upright and disinterested, prove
yourself grateful and tender-hearted; and then you will be
the perfect model of a woman.' [Fanny Price]
                                   (Edmund Bertram), *Ib.*, III.4

'Good-humoured, unaffected girls, will not do for a man
who has been used to sensible women.'   *Ib.*

Emma Woodhouse, handsome, clever, and rich, with a
comfortable home and happy disposition, seemed to unite
some of the best blessings of existence.   *Emma*, I.1

Mrs Bates, the widow of a former vicar of Highbury, was a
very old lady, almost past every thing but tea and quadrille.
                                                     Ib., I.3

Her daughter enjoyed a most uncommon degree of
popularity for a woman neither young, handsome, rich nor
married. [Miss Bates]   *Ib.*

She was a great talker upon little matters.   *Ib.*

'No man can be a good judge of the comfort a woman feels
in the society of one of her own sex.'

(Mrs Weston), *Ib.*, I.5

'Such an eye! – the true hazel eye – and so brilliant!' [Emma
Woodhouse]   *Ib.*

'One hears sometimes of a child being "the picture of
health;" now Emma always gives me the idea of being the
complete picture of grown-up health.'   *Ib.*

'She is a woman that one may, that one *must* laugh at; but
that one would not wish to slight.' [Miss Bates]

(Frank Churchill), *Ib.*, II.12

'Nobody is afraid of her: that is a great charm.' [Miss Bates]

(Emma Woodhouse), *Ib.*, I.10

'How did you think Miss Fairfax looking?'
    'Ill, very ill – that is, if a young lady can ever be allowed
to look ill.'

(Emma Woodhouse & Frank Churchill), *Ib.*, II.6

The ladies here probably exchanged looks which
meant,'Men never know when things are dirty or not;' and
the gentlemen perhaps thought each to himself,'Women
will have their little nonsenses and needless cares.'

Ib., II.11

He knew her illnesses; they never occurred but for her own
convenience.   *Ib.*, II.12

Mrs Elton, as elegant as lace and pearls could make her.

Ib., II.16

'Young ladies are delicate plants. They should take care of
their health and their complexion.'   (Mr Woodhouse), *Ib.*

'Young ladies are very sure to be cared for.'   *Ib.*

'It is only by seeing women in their own homes, among
their own set, just as they always are, that you can form any
just judgment.'

(Frank Churchill), *Ib.*, III.7

Goldsmith tells us, that when lovely woman stoops to folly, she has nothing to do but to die; and when she stoops to be disagreeable, it is equally to be recommended as a clearer of ill-fame. *Ib.,* III.9

This sweetest and best of all creatures, faultless in spite of all her faults. [Emma Woodhouse] *Ib.,* III.13

To look *almost* pretty, is an acquisition of higher delight to a girl who has been looking plain the first fifteen years of her life, than a beauty from her cradle can ever receive. [Catherine Morland] *Northanger Abbey,* I.1.

A woman especially, if she have the misfortune of knowing any thing, should conceal it as well as she can. *Ib.,* I.14

'Every body allows that the talent of writing agreeable letters is peculiarly female.' (Henry Tilney), *Ib.,* I.3

'The usual style of letter-writing among women is faultless, except in three particulars.'
　'And what are they?'
　'A general deficiency of subject, a total inattention to stops, and a very frequent ignorance of grammar.'
(Henry Tilney & Catherine Morland), *Ib.*

'I think very highly of the understanding of all the women in the world – especially of those – whoever they may be – with whom I happen to be in company.'
(Henry Tilney), *Ib.,* I.14

'No one can think more highly of the understanding of women than I do. In my opinion, nature has given them so much, that they never find it necessary to use more than half.' *Ib.*

It sometimes happens, that a woman is handsomer at twenty-nine than she was ten years before; and, generally speaking, if there has been neither ill health nor anxiety, it is a time of life at which scarcely any charm is lost.
Persuasion, I.1

A lady, without a family, was the very best preserver of furniture in the world. *Ib.,* I.3

She was young, and certainly altogether well-looking, and possessed, in an acute mind and assiduous pleasing manners, infinitely more dangerous attractions than any merely personal might have been. [Mrs Clay]   *Ib.*, I.5

'It is a thing of course among us, that every man is refused till he offers.'   (Mrs Smith), *Ib.*, II.9

'We certainly do not forget you, so soon as you forget us.'
                                                       (Anne Elliot), *Ib.*, II.11

'We live at home, quiet, confined, and our feelings prey upon us. You are forced on exertion. You have always a profession, pursuits, business of some sort or other, to take you back into the world.'   *Ib.*

'Songs and proverbs, all talk of woman's fickleness. But perhaps you will say, these were all written by men.'
                                                       (Captain Harville), *Ib.*

'A strong sense of duty is no bad part of a woman's portion.'   (Anne Elliot), *Ib.*

He had counted eighty-seven women go by, one after another, without there being a tolerable face among them. It had been a frosty morning, to be sure, a sharp frost, which hardly one woman in a thousand could stand the test of. [Sir Walter Elliot]   *Ib.*, II.3

'Do you ride?'
     'No my Lord.'
     'I wonder every lady does not. – A woman never looks better than on horseback.'
     'But every woman may not have the inclination, or the means.'
     'If they knew how much it became them, they would all have the inclination, and I fancy Miss Watson – when once they had the inclination, the means would soon follow.'
                         (Lord Osborne & Emma Watson), *The Watsons*

Mrs Portman is not much admired in Dorsetshire; the good-natured world, as usual, extolled her beauty so highly, that all the neighbourhood have had the pleasure of being disappointed.
                                                       Letters, 17 November 1798

One does not care for girls till they are grown up.

Ib., 9 September 1814

Single women have a dreadful propensity for being poor – which is one very strong argument in favour of matrimony.

Ib., 13 March 1817

Gentlemen

He was not an ill-disposed young man, unless to be rather cold hearted, and rather selfish, is to be ill-disposed. [John Dashwood]

Sense and Sensibility, 1.1

His appearance however was not unpleasing, in spite of his being in the opinion of Marianne and Margaret an absolute old bachelor, for he was on the wrong side of five and thirty. [Colonel Brandon]   *Ib.*, I.7

'Brandon is just the kind of man,' said Willoughby one day, when they were talking of him together, 'whom every body speaks well of, and nobody cares about; whom all are delighted to see, and nobody remembers to talk to.'

Ib., I.10

Benevolent, philanthropic man! It was painful to him even to keep a third cousin to himself. [Sir John Middleton]

Ib., I.21

'That is what a young man ought to be. Whatever be his pursuits, his eagerness in them should know no moderation, and leave him no sense of fatigue.'

(Marianne Dashwood), *Ib.*, I.9

Mr Palmer maintained the common, but unfatherly opinion among his sex, of all infants being alike.

Ib., II.14

'Can he be a sensible man, sir?'

'No, my dear; I think not. I have great hopes of finding him quite the reverse. There is a mixture of servility and self importance in his letter, which promises well. I am impatient to see him.' [Mr Collins]

(Elizabeth & Mr Bennet), *Pride and Prejudice*, I.13

His appearance was greatly in his favour, he had all the best part of beauty. [Mr Wickham]   *Ib.*, I.15

Mr Wickham was the happy man towards whom almost every female eye was turned, and Elizabeth the happy woman by whom he finally seated himself.   *Ib.*, I.16

'There is something of dignity in his countenance, that would not give one an unfavourable idea of his heart.' [Mr Darcy]   (Mrs Gardiner), *Ib.*, III.1

'He is as fine a fellow,' said Mr Bennet, as soon as they were out of the house, 'as ever I saw. He simpers, and smirks, and makes love to us all. I am prodigiously proud of him.' [Mr Wickham]   *Ib.*, III.11

'It looks just like that man that used to be with him before. Mr what's his name. That tall, proud man.'

'Good gracious! Mr Darcy! – and so it does I vow. Well, any friend of Mr Bingley's will always be welcome here to be sure; but else I must say that I hate the very sight of him.'

(Kitty & Mrs Bennet), *Ib.*

Bingley was every thing that was charming, except the professed lover of her daughter.   *Ib.*, III.13

Nor could he refrain from often saying to himself, in Mr Rushworth's company, 'If this man had not twelve thousand a year, he would be a very stupid fellow.'

(Edmund Bertram), *Mansfield Park*, I.4

'I think it ought not to be set down as certain, that a man must be acceptable to every woman he may happen to like himself.'   (Fanny Price), *Ib.*, III.4

Henry Crawford, ruined by early independence and bad domestic example, indulged in the freaks of a cold-blooded vanity a little too long.   *Ib.*, III.17

Mr Frank Churchill was one of the boasts of Highbury, and
a lively curiosity to see him prevailed, though the
compliment was so little returned that he had never been
there in his life.   *Emma*, I.2

'He is a man whom I cannot presume to praise.' [Mr
Knightley]   (Frank Churchill), *Ib.*, III.18

'Miss W. calls me the child of good fortune.'
                                  (Frank Churchill), *Ib.*, III.14

'Where a man does his best with only moderate powers, he
will have the advantage over negligent superiority.'
                                  (Emma Woodhouse), *Ib.*, I.13

'There is, I believe, in many men, especially single men,
such an inclination – such a passion for dining out – a
dinner engagement is so high in the class of their pleasures,
their employments, their dignities, almost their duties, that
any thing gives way to it.'   *Ib.*

'It is a great deal more natural than one could wish, that a
young man, brought up by those who are proud, luxurious,
and selfish, should be proud, luxurious, and selfish too.'
[Frank Churchill]

                                  (Mr Knightley), *Ib.*, I.18

'There is one thing, Emma, which a man can always do, if
he chuses, and that is, his duty.'   *Ib.*

'Your amiable young man can be amiable only in French,
not in English.'   *Ib.*

'Is he – is he a tall man?'
    'Who shall answer that question?' cried Emma. 'My
father would say "yes," Mr Knightley, "no;" and Miss Bates
and I that he is just the happy medium. When you have
been here a little longer, Miss Fairfax, you will understand
that Mr Elton is the standard of perfection in Highbury,
both in person and mind.'   (Emma Woodhouse) *Ib.*, II.3

'She will give you all the minute particulars, which only
woman's language can make interesting. – In our
communications we deal only in the great.'
                                  (Mr Knightley), *Ib.*, III.18

Her father was a clergyman, without being neglected, or poor, and a very respectable man, though his name was Richard – and he had never been handsome.
Northanger Abbey, I.1

I will only add in justice to men that though to the larger and more trifling part of the sex, imbecility in females is a great enhancement of their personal charms, there is a portion of them too reasonable and too well informed themselves to desire any thing more in woman than ignorance.   *Ib.*, I.14

Vanity was the beginning and the end of Sir Walter Elliot's character.   *Persuasion*, I.1

He considered the blessing of beauty as inferior only to the blessing of a baronetcy; and the Sir Walter Elliot, who united these gifts, was the constant object of his warmest respect and devotion. [Sir Walter Elliot]   *Ib.*

He had, in fact, though his sisters were now doing all they could for him, by calling him 'poor Richard,' been nothing better than a thick-headed, unfeeling, unprofitable Dick Musgrove.   *Ib.*, I.6

'He was careless and immethodical, like other men.'
(Mrs Smith), *Ib.*, II.9

'I will not allow it to be more man's nature than woman's to be inconstant.'
(Captain Harville), *Ib.*, II.11

'Man is more robust than woman, but he is not longer-lived; which exactly explains my view of the nature of their attachments.'
(Anne Elliot), *Ib.*

Wisdom & Wit

On every formal visit a child ought to be of the party, by way of provision for discourse.   *Sense and Sensibility,* I.6

Colonel Brandon alone, of all the party, heard her without being in raptures. He paid her only the compliment of attention.   *Ib.,* I.7

She was reasonable enough to allow that a man of five and thirty might well have outlived all acuteness of feeling and every exquisite power of enjoyment.   *Ib.*

'People always live for ever when there is any annuity to be paid them.'   (Mrs John Dashwood), *Ib.,* I.2

'There is something so amiable in the prejudices of a young mind that one is sorry to see them give way to the reception of more general opinions.'
   (Colonel Brandon), *Ib.,* I.11

'An annuity is a serious business.'
   (John Dashwood) *Ib.,* I.2

'What have wealth or grandeur to do with happiness?'
   'Grandeur has but little,' said Elinor, 'but wealth has much to do with it.'
   (Elinor & Marianne Dashwood), *Ib.,* I.17

'Shyness is only the effect of a sense of inferiority in some way or other.'   (Edward Ferrars), *Ib.*

'When a woman has five grown up daughters, she ought to give over thinking of her own beauty.'
   'In such cases, a woman has not often much beauty to think of.'   (Mr & Mrs Bennet), *Pride and Prejudice,* I.1

'Nothing is more deceitful,' said Darcy, 'than the appearance of humility. It is often only carelessness of opinion, and sometimes an indirect boast.'   *Ib.,* I.10

'They are young in the ways of the world, and not yet open to the mortifying conviction that handsome young men must have something to live on, as well as the plain.'

(Elizabeth Bennet), *Ib.*, II.3

'We neither of us perform to strangers.'

(Mr Darcy), *Ib.*, II.8

'Daughters are never of so much consequence to a father.'

(Lady Catherine De Bourgh), *Ib.*, II.14

'There is but such a quantity of merit between them; just enough to make one good sort of man; and of late it has been shifting about pretty much.' [Mr Wickham & Mr Darcy]

(Elizabeth Bennet), *Ib.*, II.18

'One cannot be always laughing at a man without now and then stumbling on something witty.'

Ib.

'General disappointment is only warded off by the defence of some little peculiar vexation.'

Ib., II.19

This was a lucky recollection – it saved her from something like regret.

Ib., III.1

What praise is more valuable than the praise of an intelligent servant?

Ib.

'Perhaps she *meant* well, but, under such a misfortune as this one cannot see too little of one's neighbours.'

(Elizabeth Bennet), *Ib.*

'I do not pretend to equal frankness with your ladyship. You may ask questions, which *I* shall not choose to answer.'

Ib., III.14

'I have not been in the habit of brooking disappointment.' '*That* will make your ladyship's situation at present more pitiable; but it will have no effect on *me*.'

(Lady Catherine De Bourgh & Elizabeth Bennet), *Ib.*

'You are not going to be *Missish*, I hope.'

(Mr Bennet), *Ib.*, III.15

'For what do we live, but to make sport for our neighbours,
and laugh at them in our turn?'   *Ib.*

She remembered that he had yet to learn to be laught at,
and it was rather too early to begin.

Ib., III.16

By Elizabeth's instructions she began to comprehend that a
woman may take liberties with her husband, which a
brother will not always allow in a sister more than ten years
younger than himself.   *Ib.*, III.19

'You know enough of my *frankness* to believe me capable of
that. After abusing you so abominably to your face, I could
have no scruple in abusing you to all your relations.'

(Elizabeth Bennet), *Ib.*, III.16

There are certainly not so many men of large fortune in the
world, as there are pretty women to deserve them.

Mansfield Park, I.1

'If one scheme of happiness fails, human nature turns to
another.'   (Mrs Grant), *Ib.*, I.5

'My cousin is grown up. She has the age and sense of a
woman, but the outs and not outs are beyond me.'

(Edmund Bertram), *Ib.*

A young party is always provided with a shady lane.

Ib., I.7

'The metropolis, I imagine, is a pretty fair sample of the
rest.'
    'Not, I should hope, of the proportion of virtue to vice
throughout the kingdom.'

(Mary Crawford & Edmund Bertram), *Ib.*, I.9

'As the clergy are, or are not what they ought to be, so are
the rest of the nation.'

(Edmund Bertram), *Ib.*

'You are too much a man of the world not to see with the
eyes of the world.'

(Maria Bertram), *Ib.*, I.10

His dogs, his jealousy of his neighbours, his doubts of their qualification, and his zeal after poachers – subjects which will not find their way to female feelings without some talent on one side, or some attachment on the other.

Ib., I.12

'Those who have not more, must be satisfied with what they have.' (Mrs Rushworth), *Ib.*

The value of an event on a wet day in the country, was most forcibly brought before her. *Ib.*, II.4

'I see no wonder in this shrubbery equal to seeing myself in it.' (Mary Crawford), *Ib.*

'There is a beauty in every family. – It is a regular thing.'
Ib., II.11

Sir Thomas was most cordially anxious for the perfection of Mr Crawford's character in that point. He wished him to be a model of constancy; and fancied the best means of effecting it would be by not trying him too long. *Ib.*, III.4

A wet Sunday evening – the very time of all others when if a friend is at hand the heart must be opened. *Ib.*, III.16

'It seems to have been the merciful appointment of Providence that the heart which knew no guile, should not suffer.'

(Edmund Bertram), *Ib.*

I purposely abstain from dates on this occasion, that every one may be at liberty to fix their own, aware that the cure of unconquerable passions, and the transfer of unchanging attachments, must vary much as to time in different people.
Ib., III.17

She was of course only too good for him; but as nobody minds having what is too good for them, he was very steadily earnest in the pursuit of the blessing.

Ib.

'Depend upon it, a lucky guess is never merely luck.'
(Emma Woodhouse), *Emma*, I.1

'There is no making children of three or four years old
stand still; nor can it be very easy to take any likeness of
them, beyond the air and complexion, unless they are
coarser featured than any mamma's children ever were.'
Ib., I.6

'One half of the world cannot understand the pleasures of
the other.'   *Ib.*, I.9

'It is poverty only which makes celibacy contemptible to a
generous public!'   *Ib.*, I.10

'A narrow income has a tendency to contract the mind, and
sour the temper.'   *Ib.*

'In London it is always a sickly season. Nobody is healthy
in London, nobody can be.'   (Mr Woodhouse), *Ib.*, I.12

To youth and natural cheerfulness like Emma's, though
under temporary gloom at night, the return of day will
hardly fail to bring return of spirits.   *Ib.*, I.16

A sanguine temper, though for ever expecting more good
than occurs, does not always pay for its hopes by any
proportionate depression. It soon flies over the present
failure and begins to hope again.   *Ib.*, I.18

'Nobody, who has not been in the interior of a family, can
say what the difficulties of any individual of that family
may be.'   (Emma Woodhouse), *Ib.*

'What arises from discretion must be honoured.'
(Mr Knightley), *Ib.*, II.3

'In coming *home* I felt I might do any thing.'
(Frank Churchill), *Ib.*, II.5

'What can any body's native air do for them in the months
of January, February, and March? Good fires and carriages
would be much more to the purpose.'
(Emma Woodhouse), *Ib.*, II.8

'The post-office has a great charm at one period of our lives.'
(John Knightley), *Ib.*, II.16

'Business, you know, may bring money, but friendship
hardly ever does.'   *Ib.*

It was a sweet view – sweet to the eye and the mind.
English verdure, English culture, English comfort, seen
under a sun bright, without being oppressive.   *Ib.*, III.6

Mrs Weston was ready, on the first meeting, to consider the
subject in the most serviceable light – first, as a settled, and
secondly, as a good one.   *Ib.*, III.17

She would be placed in the midst of those who loved her,
and who had better sense than herself; retired enough for
safety, and occupied enough for cheerfulness. She would
be never led into temptation, nor left for it to find her out.
[Harriet Smith]   *Ib.*, III.19

'What do you deserve?'
    'Oh! I always deserve the best treatment, because I never
put up with any other.'
                        (Mr Knightley & Emma Woodhouse), *Ib.*, III.18

'That little boys and girls should be tormented,' said Henry,
'is what no one at all acquainted with human nature in a
civilized state can deny.'
                        (Henry Tilney), *Northanger Abbey*, I.4

A family of ten children will always be called a fine family,
where there are heads and arms and legs enough for the
number.   *Ib.*, I.1

'I cannot speak well enough to be unintelligible.'
                        (Catherine Morland), *Ib.*, II.1

'Modesty, and all that, is very well in its way, but really a
little common honesty is sometimes quite as becoming.'
                        (Isabella Thorpe), *Ib.*, II.3

'I have just learnt to love a hyacinth.'
                        (Catherine Morland) *Ib.*, II.7

In the central part of England there was surely some
security for the existence even of a wife not beloved, in the
laws of the land, and the manners of the age.
                                                      Ib., II.10

'You feel, as you always do, what is most to the credit of
human nature. – Such feelings ought to be investigated,
that they may know themselves.'   (Henry Tilney), *Ib.*

'The person who has contracted debts must pay for them.'
                                  (Lady Russell), *Persuasion*, I.2

To be claimed as a good, though in an improper style, is at
least better than being rejected as no good at all.   *Ib.*, I.5

Now they were as strangers; nay, worse than strangers, for
they could never become acquainted.   *Ib.*, I.8

Personal size and mental sorrow have certainly no
necessary proportions. A large bulky figure has as good a
right to be in deep affliction, as the most graceful set of
limbs in the world.   *Ib.*

A very strange stranger it must be, who does not see
charms in the immediate environs of Lyme.   *Ib.*, I.11

Nor could she help fearing, on more serious reflection, that,
like many other great moralists and preachers, she had
been eloquent on a point in which her own conduct would
ill bear examination. [Anne Elliot]   *Ib.*

A persuadable temper might sometimes be as much in
favour of happiness, as a very resolute character.
                                                    Ib., I.12

'One man's ways may be as good as another's, but we all
like our own best.'   (Admiral Croft), *Ib.*, II.1

Every body has their taste in noises as well as in other
matters; and sounds are quite innoxious, or most
distressing, by their sort rather than their quantity.
                                                    Ib., II.2

If he really sought to reconcile himself like a dutiful branch,
he must be forgiven for having dismembered himself from
the paternal tree.   *Ib.*

'A sick chamber may often furnish the worth of volumes.'
                                  (Anne Elliot), *Ib.*, II.5

'Like other great men under reverses,' he added with a smile, 'I must endeavour to subdue my mind to my fortune. I must learn to brook being happier than I deserve.'

(Captain Wentworth), *Ib.*, II.11

There is a quickness of perception in some, a nicety in the discernment of character, a natural penetration, in short, which no experience in others can equal. *Ib.*, II.12

To flatter and follow others, without being flattered and followed in turn, is but a state of half enjoyment. *Ib.*

Every neighbourhood should have a great Lady.

Sanditon, 3

'Those who tell their own story you know must be listened to with caution.' (Mr Parker), *Ib.*

'Our ancestors, you know, always built in a hole.' *Ib.*, 4

I do not want people to be very agreeable, as it saves me the trouble of liking them a great deal.

Letters, 24 December 1798

Your letter is come; it came indeed twelve lines ago, but I could not stop to acknowledge it before, and I am glad it did not arrive till I had completed my first sentence, because the sentence had been made ever since yesterday, and I think forms a very good beginning.

Ib., 1 November 1800

I give you joy of our new nephew, and hope if he ever comes to be hanged, it will not be till we are too old to care about it. *Ib.*, 25 April 1811

So young and so blooming and so innocent, as if she had never had a wicked thought in her life – which yet one has some reason to suppose she must have had, if we believe the doctrine of original sin.

Ib., 20 February 1817

I must not depend upon being ever very blooming again. Sickness is a dangerous indulgence at my time of life.

Ib., 23 March 1817

Wisdom is better than Wit, and in the long run will
certainly have the laugh on her side.
Ib., 18 November 1814

Elegance & Grace

His private balls were numerous enough for any young
lady who was not suffering under the insatiable appetite of
fifteen.
Sense and Sensibility, 1.7

'Every savage can dance.'
(Mr Darcy), *Pride and Prejudice*, I.6

'It would surely be much more rational if conversation
instead of dancing made the order of the day.'
   'Much more rational, my dear Caroline, I dare say but it
would not be near so much like a ball.'
(Caroline & Mr Bingley), *Ib.*, I.11

He argued like a young man very much bent on dancing.
[Frank Churchill]   *Emma*, II.6

It may be possible to do without dancing entirely. Instances
have been known of young people passing many, many
months successively, without being at any ball of any
description, and no material injury accrue either to body or
mind.   *Ib.*, II.11

'Nothing can be farther from pleasure than to be dancing in
a crowd – and a crowd in a little room.'
(Emma Woodhouse), *Ib.*

A private dance, without sitting down to supper, was
pronounced an infamous fraud upon the rights of men and
women.   *Ib.*

'Fine dancing, I believe, like virtue, must be its own reward.'
(Mr Knightley), *Ib.*, II.12

'I consider a country-dance as an emblem of marriage. Fidelity and complaisance are the principal duties of both; and those men who do not chuse to dance or marry themselves, have no business with the partners or wives of their neighbours.'

(Henry Tilney), *Northanger Abbey*, I.10

Dress is at all times a frivolous distinction, and excessive solicitude about it often destroys its own aim.

Ib.

Man only can be aware of the insensibility of man towards a new gown.

Ib.

Woman is fine for her own satisfaction alone. No man will admire her the more, no woman will like her the better for it. Neatness and fashion are enough for the former, and a something of shabbiness or impropriety will be most endearing to the latter.

Ib.

I am almost afraid to tell you how my Irish friend and I behaved. Imagine to yourself everything most profligate and shocking in the way of dancing and sitting down together.

Letters, 9 January 1796

What dreadful hot weather we have! – It keeps one in a continual state of inelegance.

Letters, 18 September 1796

'Your sentiments so nobly expressed on the different excellencies of Indian and English muslins, and the judicious preference you give the former, have excited in me an admiration of which I can alone give an adequate idea by assuring you it is nearly equal to what I feel for myself.'

(Charlotte & Elfrida), *Frederica and Elfrida*, 2

Love

A man could not very well be in love with either of her daughters, without extending the passion to her. [Mrs Dashwood]

Sense and Sensibility, I.17

'Who did I ever hear him talk of as young and attractive among his female acquaintance? – Oh! no one, no one – he talked to me only of myself.'

(Marianne Dashwood) *Ib.*, II.7

Had not Elinor, in the sad countenance of her sister, seen a check to all mirth, she could have been entertained by Mrs Jennings' endeavours to cure a disappointment in love by a variety of sweetmeats and olives, and a good fire.

Ib., II.8

'When a young man, be he who he will, comes and makes love to a pretty girl, and promises marriage, he has no business to fly off from his word only because he grows poor and a richer girl is ready to have him.'

(Mrs Jennings) *Ib.*

She could not help believing herself the nicest observer of the two; – she watched his eyes while Mrs Jennings thought only of his behaviour. [Colonel Brandon]

Ib., III.6

Vanity, while seeking its own guilty triumph at the expense of another, had involved him in a real attachment, which extravagance, or at least its offspring, necessity, had required to be sacrificed. [Willoughby]

Ib., III.8

After experiencing the blessings of *one* imprudent engagement, contracted without his mother's consent, as he had already done for more than four years, nothing less could be expected of him in the failure of *that*, than the immediate contraction of another. [Edward Ferrars]

Ib., III.13

Though a very few hours spent in the hard labour of incessant talking will dispatch more subjects than can really be in common between any two rational creatures, yet with lovers it is different. Between *them* no subject is finished, no communication is even made, till it has been made at least twenty times over.   *Ib.*

'I scorn to accept a hand while the heart was another's.'
(Lucy Steele) *Ib.*

Instead of talking of Edward, they came gradually to talk only of Robert, – a subject on which he had always more to say than on any other, and in which she soon betrayed an interest even equal to his own.   *Ib.*, III.14

'He admires as a lover, not as a connoisseur.'
(Marianne Dashwood), *Ib.*, I.3

'There are very few of us who have heart enough to be really in love without encouragement.'
(Charlotte Lucas), *Pride and Prejudice*, I.6

'When she is secure of him there will be leisure for falling in love as much as she chuses.'   *Ib.*

'There is meanness in *all* the arts which ladies sometimes condescend to employ for captivation.'
(Mr Darcy), *Ib.*, I.8

'To find a man agreeable whom one is determined to hate! – Do not wish me such an evil.'
(Elizabeth Bennet), *Ib.*, I.18

The idea of Mr Collins, with all his solemn composure, being run away with by his feelings, made Elizabeth so near laughing that she could not use the short pause to stop him farther.   *Ib.*, I.19

The stupidity with which he was favoured by nature, must guard his courtship from any charm that could make a woman wish for its continuance. [Mr Collins]   *Ib.*, I.22

'Women fancy admiration means more than it does.'
  'And men take care that they should.'
(Jane & Elizabeth Bennet), *Ib.*, II.1

'Your sister is crossed in love I find. I congratulate her. Next to being married, a girl likes to be crossed in love a little now and then.' (Mr Bennet), *Ib.*

'Let Wickham be *your* man. He is a pleasant fellow, and would jilt you creditably.'
 'Thank you, Sir, but a less agreeable man would satisfy me. We must not all expect Jane's good fortune.'
(Mr Bennet & Elizabeth Bennet), *Ib.*

'You are too sensible a girl, Lizzy, to fall in love merely because you are warned against it.'
(Mrs Gardiner), *Ib.*, II.3

'I had not known you a month before I felt that you were the last man in the world whom I could ever be prevailed on to marry.'
(Elizabeth Bennet), *Ib.*, II.11

'Well, my comfort is, I am sure Jane will die of a broken heart, and then he will be sorry for what he has done.'
(Mrs Bennet), *Ib.*, II.17

Never had she so honestly felt that she could have loved him, as now, when all love must be vain. *Ib.*, III.4

'I thought him very sly; – he hardly ever mentioned your name. But slyness seems the fashion.'
(Mrs Gardiner), *Ib.*, III.10

'Is there one among the sex, who would not protest against such a weakness as a second proposal to the same woman?'
(Elizabeth Bennet), *Ib.*, III.12

He expressed himself on the occasion as sensibly and as warmly as a man violently in love can be supposed to do.
[Mr Darcy] *Ib.*, III.16

'Perhaps I did not always love him so well as I do now. But in such cases as these, a good memory is unpardonable. This is the last time I shall ever remember it myself.'
(Elizabeth Bennet), *Ib.*, III.17

'It is settled between us already. We are to be the happiest couple in the world.' *Ib.*

'Will you tell me how long you have loved him?'

'It has been coming on so gradually, that I hardly know when it began. But I believe I must date it from my first seeing his beautiful grounds at Pemberley.'

(Jane & Elizabeth Bennet), Ib.

'These violent young lovers carry everything their own way.' (Mr Bennet), Ib.

'If any young men come for Mary or Kitty, send them in, for I am quite at leisure.' Ib.

'I am happier even than Jane; she only smiles, I laugh.'
(Elizabeth Bennet), Ib., III.18

'Mr Darcy sends you all the love in the world, that he can spare from me.' Ib.

Mr Rushworth was from the first struck with the beauty of Miss Bertram, and being inclined to marry, soon fancied himself in love. Mansfield Park, I.4

'I think too well of Miss Bertram to suppose she would ever give her hand without her heart.'
(Henry Crawford), Ib., I.5

Every thing will turn to account when love is once set going, even the sandwich tray. Ib., I.7

Henry Crawford had destroyed her happiness, but he should not know that he had done it; he should not destroy her credit, her appearance, her prosperity too. Ib., II.3

'And so this is her attraction after all! This it is – her not caring about you – which gives her such a soft skin and makes her so much taller.' (Mary Crawford), Ib., II.6

The enthusiasm of a woman's love is even beyond the biographer's. Ib., II.9

'Is not there a something wanted, Miss Price, in our language – a something between compliments and – and love – to suit the sort of friendly acquaintance we have had together?'

(Mary Crawford), Ib., II.11

'We must have walked at least a mile in this wood. Do you not think we have?'

'Not half a mile,' was his sturdy answer; for he was not yet so much in love as to measure distance, or reckon time, with feminine lawlessness.

(Mary Crawford & Edmund Bertram), *Ib.*, I.9

'I never have been in love; it is not my way, or my nature.'
(Emma Woodhouse), *Emma*, I.10

'Any thing interests between those who love; and any thing will serve as introduction to what is near the heart.'   *Ib.*

Harriet was one of those, who, having once begun, would be always in love.   *Ib.*, II.4

'He is so very much occupied by the idea of *not* being in love with her, that I should not wonder if it were to end in his being so at last.'   (Mrs Weston), *Ib.*, II.15

He had found her agitated and low. – Frank Churchill was a villain. – He heard her declare that she had never loved him. Frank Churchill's character was not desperate. – She was his own Emma, by hand and word, when they returned into the house; and if he could have thought of Frank Churchill then, he might have deemed him a very good sort of fellow.   *Ib.*, III.13

'I refer every caviller to a brick house, sashed windows below, and casements above, in Highbury.'
(Frank Churchill), *Ib.*, III.14

'My heart was in Highbury, and my business was to get my body thither as often as might be.'   *Ib.*

'There is safety in reserve, but no attraction. One cannot love a reserved person.'

'Not till the reserve ceases towards oneself; and then the attraction may be the greater.'
(Frank Churchill & Emma Woodhouse), *Ib.*, II.6

It really was too much to hope even of Harriet, that she could be in love with more than *three* men in one year.
Ib., III.15

Such a heart – such a Harriet!   *Ib.*, III.18

If it be true, as a celebrated writer has maintained, that no young lady can be justified in falling in love before the gentleman's love is declared, it must be very improper that a young lady should dream of a gentleman before the gentleman is first known to have dreamt of her.

Northanger Abbey, I.3

Friendship is certainly the finest balm for the pangs of disappointed love.   *Ib.*, I.4

All have been, or at least all have believed themselves to be, in danger from the pursuit of some one whom they wished to avoid; and all have been anxious for the attentions of some one whom they wished to please.

Ib., I.10

Where people wish to attach, they should always be ignorant. To come with a well-informed mind, is to come with an inability of administering to the vanity of others, which a sensible person would always wish to avoid.

Ib., I.14

'I hate the idea of one great fortune looking out for another.'
(Catherine Morland), *Ib.*, I.15

Listening with sparkling eyes to everything he said; and, in finding him irresistible, becoming so herself. [Catherine Morland]   *Ib.*, II.1

'No man is offended by another man's admiration of the woman he loves; it is the woman only who can make it a torment.'   (Henry Tilney), *Ib.*, II.4

I must confess that his affection originated in nothing better than gratitude, or, in other words, that a persuasion of her partiality for him had been the only cause of giving her a serious thought. It is a new circumstance in romance, I acknowledge, and dreadfully derogatory of an heroine's dignity; but if it be as new in common life, the credit of a wild imagination will at least be all my own.

Ib., II.15

Alas! with all her reasonings, she found, that to retentive feelings eight years may be little more than nothing.

Persuasion, I.7

'If I loved a man, as she loves the Admiral, I would be always with him, nothing should ever separate us, and I would rather be overturned by him, than driven safely by anybody else.'

(Louisa Musgrove), *Ib.*, I.10

'Every body's heart is open, you know, when they have recently escaped from severe pain, or are recovering the blessing of health.'

(Mrs Smith), *Ib.*, II.5

'A man does not recover from such a devotion of the heart to such a woman! – He ought not – he does not.'

(Captain Wentworth), *Ib.*, II.8

Her union, she believed, could not divide her more from other men, than their final separation. *Ib.*, II.9

'I have been rather too much used to the game to be soon overcome by a gentleman's hints.'

(Miss Elliot), *Ib.*, II.10

'All the privilege I claim for my own sex (it is not a very enviable one, you need not covet) is that of loving longest, when existence or when hope is gone.'

(Anne Elliot), *Ib.*, II.11

'Dare not say that man forgets sooner than woman, that his love has an earlier death. I have loved none but you.'

(Captain Wentworth), *Ib.*

The power of conversation would make the present hour a blessing indeed; and prepare for it all the immortality which the happiest recollections of their own future lives could bestow. *Ib.*

All the little variations of the last week were gone through; and of yesterday and to-day there could scarcely be an end.

Ib.

The expence alas! of measures in that masterly style was ill-suited to his purse, and prudence obliged him to prefer the quietest sort of ruin and disgrace for the object of his affections, to the more renowned. [Sir Edward Denham]

Sanditon, 8

'There is no resisting a cockade my dear.'
  'I hope there is.' – said Mrs E. gravely, with a quick
glance at her daughter.

(Mr & Mrs Edwardes), The Watsons

'Carefulness – discretion – should not be confined to
elderly ladies, or to a second choice' added his wife. 'It is
quite as necessary to young ladies in their first.'
  'Rather more so, my dear' – replied he, 'because young
ladies are likely to feel the effects of it longer.'

Ib.

'I have never yet found that the advice of a sister could
prevent a young man's being in love if he chose it.'

(Lady Susan Vernon), Lady Susan

'Her feelings are tolerably lively, and she is so charmingly
artless in their display, as to afford the most reasonable
hope of her being ridiculed and despised by every man
who sees her.'

Ib.

His regard, which appeared to spring from knowing
nothing of me at first, is best supported by never seeing me.

Letters, 17 November 1798

I feel the sterling worth of such a young man & the
desirableness of your growing in love with him again. I
recommend this most thoroughly.

Ib., 18 November 1814

'He is extremely disagreeable and I hate him more than any
body else in the world. He has a large fortune and will
make great settlements on me; but then he is very healthy.
In short I do not know what to do.'

(Miss Stanhope), The Three Sisters

Marriage

They strongly resembled each other in that total want of talent and taste which confined their employments, unconnected with such as society produced, within a very narrow compass. [Sir John & Lady Middleton]

Sense and Sensibility, I.7

'Thirty-five has nothing to do with matrimony.'
    'Perhaps,' said Elinor, 'thirty-five and seventeen had better not have any thing to do with matrimony together.'

(Marianne & Elinor Dashwood), *Ib.*, I.8

He did not, upon the whole, expect a very cruel reception. It was his business, however, to say that he *did*, and he said it very prettily. What he might say on the subject a twelvemonth after, must be referred to the imagination of husbands and wives.
Ib., III.13

His temper might perhaps be a little soured by finding, like many others of his sex, that through some unaccountable bias in favour of beauty, he was the husband of a very silly woman. [Mr Palmer]
Ib., I.20

'Oh! dear! one never thinks of married mens' being beaux – they have something else to do.'

(Miss Steele), *Ib.*, I.21

It would be an excellent match, for *he* was rich and *she* was handsome.
Ib., I.8

It is a truth universally acknowledged, that a single man in possession of a good fortune, must be in want of a wife.
Pride and Prejudice, I.1

'It is better to know as little as possible of the defects of the person with whom you are to pass your life.'

(Charlotte Lucas), *Ib.*, I.6

'A lady's imagination is very rapid; it jumps from admiration to love, from love to matrimony in a moment.'

(Mr Darcy), *Ib.*

'An unhappy alternative is before you, Elizabeth. From this day you must be a stranger to one of your parents. – Your mother will never see you again if you do *not* marry Mr Collins, and I will never see you again if you *do*.'

(Mr Bennet), *Ib.*, I.20

'If upon mature deliberation, you find that the misery of disobliging his two sisters is more than equivalent to the happiness of being his wife, I advise you by all means to refuse him.'   (Elizabeth Bennet), *Ib.*, I.21

The strangeness of Mr Collins's making two offers of marriage within three days, was nothing in comparison of his being now accepted.   *Ib.*, I.22

'And pray, what is the usual price of an Earl's younger son? Unless the elder brother is very sickly, I suppose you would not ask above fifty thousand pounds.'

(Elizabeth Bennet), *Ib.*, II.10

To his wife he was very little otherwise indebted, than as her ignorance and folly had contributed to his amusement. This is not the sort of happiness which a man would in general wish to owe to his wife; but where other powers of entertainment are wanting, the true philosopher will derive benefit from such as are given. [Mr Bennet]   *Ib.*, II.19

She was more alive to the disgrace, which the want of new clothes must reflect on her daughter's nuptials, than to any sense of shame at her eloping and living with Wickham, a fortnight before they took place.   *Ib.*, III.18

Miss Bingley's congratulations to her brother, on his approaching marriage, were all that was affectionate and insincere.   *Ib.*

Happy for all her maternal feelings was the day on which Mrs Bennet got rid of her two most deserving daughters.

Ib., III.19

She felt all the injuries of beauty in Mrs Grant's being so well settled in life without being handsome.

Mansfield Park, I.3

Matrimony was her object.   *Ib.*, I.4

'If you can persuade Henry to marry, you must have the address of a French-woman. All that English abilities can do, has been tried already.'

(Mary Crawford), *Ib.*

'There is not one in a hundred of either sex, who is not taken in when they marry.' *Ib.*, I.5

In all the important preparations of the mind she was complete; being prepared for matrimony by an hatred of home, restraint, and tranquillity; by the misery of disappointed affection, and contempt of the man she was to marry. The rest might wait. [Maria Bertram]

Ib., II.3

No one could have supposed, from her confident triumph, that she had ever heard of conjugal infelicity in her life. [Mrs Norris] *Ib.*

The Admiral hated marriage, and thought it never pardonable in a young man of independent fortune.

Ib., II.12

How wretched, and how unpardonable, how hopeless and how wicked it was, to marry without affection. *Ib.*, III.1

'He will make you happy, Fanny, I know he will make you happy; but you will make him every thing.'

(Edmund Bertram), *Ib.*, III.4

'The glory of fixing one who has been shot by so many; of having it in one's power to pay off the debts of one's sex!'

(Mary Crawford), *Ib.*, III.5

'His fault, the liking to make girls a little in love with him, is not half so dangerous to a wife's happiness, as a tendency to fall in love himself.' [Henry Crawford] *Ib.*

Matrimony, as the origin of change, was always disagreeable.

Emma, I.5

She had a husband whose warm heart and sweet temper made him think every thing due to her in return for the great goodness of being in love with him.

Ib., I.2

'I lay it down as a general rule, Harriet, that if a woman *doubts* as to whether she should accept a man or not, she certainly ought to refuse him.'

(Emma Woodhouse), *Ib.*, I.7

'A woman is not to marry a man merely because she is asked, or because he is attached to her, and can write a tolerable letter.' *Ib.*

'It is always incomprehensible to a man that a woman should ever refuse an offer of marriage. A man always imagines a woman to be ready for anybody who asks her.'

Ib., I.8

'Men of sense, whatever you may chuse to say, do not want silly wifes.'

(Mr Knightley), *Ib.*

'Harriet Smith is a girl who will marry somebody or other.'

Ib.

That chance, that luck which so often defies anticipation in matrimonial affairs, giving attraction to what is moderate rather than to what is superior.

Ib., II.2

It seemed as if he could not think so ill of any two persons' understanding as to suppose they meant to marry till it were proved against them. [Mr Woodhouse]

Ib., II.5

Mrs Elton was first seen at church: but though devotion might be interrupted, curiosity could not be satisfied by a bride in a pew.

Ib., II.14

She considered how peculiarly unlucky poor Mr Elton was in being in the same room at once with the woman he had just married, the woman he had wanted to marry, and the woman whom he had been expected to marry.

Ib.

The chosen, the first, the dearest, the friend, the wife to whom he looked for all the best blessings of existence.

Ib., III.12

'So early in life – at three and twenty – a period when, if a man chooses a wife, he generally chooses ill. At three and twenty to have drawn such a prize! – What years of felicity that man, in all human calculation, has before him!'

(Mr Knightley), *Ib.*, III.13

It was not to be doubted that poor Harriet's attachment had been an offering to conjugal unreserve. *Ib.*, II.15

She spoke then, on being so entreated. – What did she say? – Just what she ought, of course. A lady always does.

Ib., III.13

'Here have I been sitting this hour, giving these young ladies a sample of true conjugal obedience – for who can say, you know, how soon it may be wanted?'

(Mrs Elton), *Ib.*, III.16

'Very little white satin, very few lace veils; a most pitiful business! – Selina would stare when she heard of it.'

(Mrs Elton), *Ib.*, III.19

In spite of these deficiencies, the wishes, the hopes, the confidence, the predictions of the small band of true friends who witnessed the ceremony, were fully answered in the perfect happiness of the union. *Ib.*

'A bride, you know, must appear like a bride.'

(Mrs Elton), *Ib.*, II.17

To begin perfect happiness at the respective ages of twenty-six and eighteen, is to do pretty well.

Northanger Abbey, II.16

Husbands and wives generally understand when opposition will be vain. *Persuasion*, I.7

'In marrying a man indifferent to me, all risk would have been incurred, and all duty violated.'

(Anne Elliot), *Ib.*, II.11

When any two young people take it into their heads to marry, they are pretty sure by perseverance to carry their point, be they ever so poor, or ever so imprudent, or ever so little likely to be necessary to each other's ultimate comfort.

Ib., II.12

'I would rather be Teacher at a school (and I can think of nothing worse) than marry a man I did not like.'
'I would rather do any thing than be Teacher at a school' – said her sister.   (Emma & Miss Watson), *The Watsons*

'My dear Alicia, of what a mistake were you guilty in marrying a man of his age! – just old enough to be formal, ungovernable and to have the gout – too old to be agreeable, and too young to die.'

(Lady Susan Vernon), *Lady Susan*

Anything is to be preferred or endured rather than marrying without Affection.   Letters, 18 November 1814

You like him well enough to marry, but not well enough to wait.   *Ib.*, 30 November 1814

Folly & Vice

'If their praise is censure, your censure may be praise, for they are not more undiscerning, than you are prejudiced and unjust.'

(Elinor Dashwood), *Sense and Sensibility*, I.10

'Oh!' cried Marianne, 'with what transporting sensations have I formerly seen them fall! How have I delighted as I walked, to see them driven in showers about me by the wind! What feelings have they, the season, the air altogether inspired! Now there is no one to regard them. They are seen only as a nuisance swept hastily off, and driven as much as possible from the sight.'
'It is not every one,' said Elinor, 'who has your passion for dead leaves.'   *Ib.*, I.16

The Dashwoods were so prodigiously delighted with the Middletons, that though not much in the habit of giving anything, they determined to give them – a dinner.

Ib., II.12

Almost all laboured under one or other of these disqualifications for being agreeable – Want of sense, either natural or improved – want of elegance – want of spirits – or want of temper. *Ib.*

Fortunately for those who pay their court through such foibles, a fond mother, though, in pursuit of praise for her children, the most rapacious of human beings, is likewise the most credulous. *Ib.*, I.21

' "My dear Madam," I always say to her, "you must make yourself easy. The evil is irremediable, and it has been entirely your own doing." ' (Robert Ferrars), *Ib.*, II.14

Elinor agreed to it all, for she did not think he deserved the compliment of rational opposition. *Ib.*

'I do not mean to justify myself, but at the same time cannot leave you to suppose that I have nothing to urge – that because she was injured she was irreproachable, and because I was a libertine, *she* must be a saint.'
(Willoughby), *Ib.*, III.8

Elinor scolded him, harshly as ladies always scold the imprudence which compliments themselves.
Ib., III.13

'You have no compassion on my poor nerves.'
'You mistake me, my dear. I have a high respect for your nerves. They are my old friends. I have heard you mention them with consideration these twenty years at least.'
(Mr & Mrs Bennet), *Pride and Prejudice*, I.1

'I sometimes amuse myself with suggesting and arranging such little elegant compliments as may be adapted to ordinary occasions, I always wish to give them as unstudied an air as possible.'
(Mr Collins), *Ib.*, I.14

To Elizabeth it appeared, that had her family made an agreement to expose themselves as much as they could during the evening, it would have been impossible for them to play their parts with more spirit, or finer success.
Ib., I.18

'It is very hard to think that Charlotte Lucas should ever be mistress of this house, that I should be forced to make way for her, and live to see her take my place in it!'

'My dear, do not give way to such gloomy thoughts. Let us hope for better things. Let us flatter ourselves that *I* may be the survivor.' (Mr & Mrs Bennet), *Ib.*, I.23

'If it was not for the entail I should not mind it.'

'What should you not mind?'

'I should not mind any thing at all.'

'Let us be thankful that you are preserved from a state of such insensibility.' *Ib.*

They were ignorant, idle, and vain. While there was an officer in Meryton, they would flirt with him; and while Meryton was within a walk of Longbourn, they would be going there for ever. *Ib.*, II.15

'You have delighted us long enough.'

(Mr Bennet), *Ib.*, I.18

'Well, well,' said he, 'do not make yourself unhappy. If you are a good girl for the next ten years, I will take you to a review at the end of them.'

(Mr Bennet), *Ib.*, III.6

She sat down, resolving within herself, to draw no limits in future to the impudence of an impudent man.

Ib., III.9

'You ought certainly to forgive them as a christian, but never to admit them in your sight.' (Mr Collins), *Ib.*, III.15

'Such a charming man! – so handsome! so tall! – Oh, my dear Lizzy! pray apologise for my having disliked him so much before. I hope he will overlook it.'

(Mrs Bennet), *Ib.*, III.17

It appeared to her, that as far as this world alone was concerned, the greatest blessing to every one of kindred with Mrs Rushworth would be instant annihilation.

Mansfield Park, III.15

He was released from the engagement to be mortified and unhappy, till some other pretty girl could attract him into matrimony again. *Ib.*, III.17

He loved to see the cloth laid, because it had been the fashion of his youth; but his conviction of suppers being very unwholesome made him rather sorry to see any thing put on it.   *Emma*, I.3

'An egg boiled very soft is not unwholesome.'
                                         (Mr Woodhouse), *Ib.*

'Hartfield pork is not like any other pork – but still it is pork.'   *Ib.*, II.3

Emma saw his spirits affected by the idea of his daughter's attachment to her husband. [Mr Woodhouse]   *Ib.*, I.9

'It seems to depend upon nothing but the ill-humour of Mrs Churchill, which I imagine to be the most certain thing in the world.'   (Emma Woodhouse), *Ib.*, I.14

'What is the certainty of caprice?'   (Mrs Weston), *Ib.*

'Her ignorance is hourly flattery.'   (Mr Knightley), *Ib.*, I.5

'You were saying something at the very moment of this burst of my *amor patriae*. Do not let me lose it. I assure you the utmost stretch of public fame would not make me amends for the loss of any happiness in private life.'
                                     (Frank Churchill), *Ib.*, II.6

'Certainly silly things do cease to be silly if they are done by sensible people in an impudent way.'
                                   (Emma Woodhouse), *Ib.*, II.8

'To have her haunting the abbey, and thanking him all day long for his great kindness in marrying Jane? – "So very kind and obliging! But he always had been such a very kind neighbour!" And then fly off, through half a sentence, to her mother's old petticoat. "Not that it was such a very old petticoat either – for still it would last a great while – and, indeed, she must thankfully say that their petticoats were all very strong." ' [Miss Bates]   *Ib.*

'Do not tell his father, but that young man is not quite the thing. He has been opening the doors very often this evening and keeping them open very inconsiderately.'
                                      (Mr Woodhouse), *Ib.*, II.11

She had an unhappy state of health in general for the child of such a man, for she hardly knew what indisposition was; and if he did not invent illnesses for her, she could make no figure in a message. [Emma Woodhouse]   *Ib.*, III.3

Could he have seen the heart, he would have cared very little for the lungs.   *Ib.*, III.14

'A thoughtless young person will sometimes step behind a window-curtain, and throw up a sash, without its being suspected. I have often known it done myself.'
   'Have you indeed, sir? – Bless me! I never could have supposed it. But I live out of the world, and am often astonished at what I hear.'
                    (Frank Churchill & Mr Woodhouse), *Ib.*, II.11

Mr Knightley seemed to be trying not to smile; and succeeded without difficulty, upon Mrs Elton's beginning to talk to him.   *Ib.*, II.18

Donwell was famous for its strawberry-beds, which seemed a plea for the invitation: but no plea was necessary; cabbage-beds would have been enough to tempt the lady.
                    Ib., III.6

'I shall be sure to say three dull things as soon as ever I open my mouth, shan't I – (looking round with the most good-humoured dependence on every body's assent) – Do not you all think I shall?'
   Emma could not resist.
   'Ah! ma'am, but there may be a difficulty. Pardon me – but you will be limited as to number – only three at once.'
                    (Miss Bates & Emma Woodhouse), *Ib.*, III.7

Their joy on this meeting was very great, as well it might since they had been contented to know nothing of each other for the last fifteen years.
                    Northanger Abbey, I.4

'Riot! – what riot?'
   'My dear Eleanor, the riot is only in your own brain.'
                    (Henry & Miss Tilney), *Ib.*, I.14

For one daughter, his eldest, he would really have given up any thing, which he had not been very much tempted to do.
                    Persuasion, I.1

Sir Walter, without hesitation, declared the Admiral to be
the best-looking sailor he had ever met with, and went so
far as to say, that, if his own man might have had the
arranging of his hair, he should not be ashamed of being
seen with him anywhere.   *Ib.*, I.5

'We do not call Bermuda or Bahama, you know, the West
Indies.'
    Mrs Musgrove had not a word to say in dissent; she
could not accuse herself of having ever called them any
thing in the whole course of her life.   (Mr Croft), *Ib.*, I.8

Many were collected near them, to be useful if wanted, at
any rate, to enjoy the sight of a dead young lady, nay, two
dead young ladies, for it proved twice as fine as the first
report.   *Ib.*, I.12

She saw that there had been bad habits; that Sunday-
travelling had been a common thing.   *Ib.*, II.5

'My sore-throats, you know, are always worse than
anybody's.'   (Mary Musgrove), *Ib.*, II.6

'A very fine young man indeed!' said Lady Dalrymple.
'More air than one often sees in Bath. – Irish, I dare say.'
                                                           Ib., II.8

The sea air and sea bathing together were nearly infallible,
one or the other of them being a match for every disorder,
of the stomach, the lungs or the blood; they were
anti-spasmodic, anti-pulmonary, anti-septic, anti-bilious
and anti-rheumatic. Nobody could catch cold by the sea,
nobody wanted appetite by the sea, nobody wanted spirits,
nobody wanted strength.   *Sanditon*, 2

'You will not think I have made a bad exchange, when we
reach Trafalgar House – which by the bye, I almost wish I
had not named Trafalgar – for Waterloo is more the thing
now.'   (Mr Parker), *Ib.*, 4

'There is a someone in most families privileged by superior
abilities or spirits to say anything.'   *Ib.*

'Thus it is, when rich people are sordid.'
                                    (Charlotte Heywood), *Ib.*, 7

Mrs Hall of Sherbourne was brought to bed yesterday of a dead child, some weeks before she expected, owing to a fright. I suppose she happened unawares to look at her husband.   Letters, 27 October 1798

I am proud to say that I have a very good eye at an adultress, for tho' repeatedly assured that another in the same party was the *She*, I fixed upon the right one from the first.   *Ib.*, 12 May 1801

Mrs Badcock thought herself obliged to leave them to run round the room after her drunken husband. His avoidance, and her pursuit, with the probable intoxication of both, was an amusing scene.   *Ib.*

Mrs Armstrong sat darning a pair of stockings the whole of my visit. But I do not mention this at home, lest a warning should act as an example.

Ib., 14 September 1804

Poor Mrs Stent! it has been her lot to be always in the way; but we must be merciful, for perhaps in time we may come to be Mrs Stents ourselves, unequal to anything & unwelcome to everybody.

Ib., 22 January 1805

I see nothing to be glad of, unless I make it a matter of joy that Mrs Wylmot has another son, and that Lord Lucan has taken a mistress, both of which events are of course joyful to the actors.

Ib., 8 February 1807

Mr Husket Lord Lansdown's painter, – domestic painter I should call him, for he lives in the castle. Domestic chaplains have given way to this more necessary office, and I suppose whenever the walls want no touching up, he is employed about my Lady's face.   *Ib.*

I am rather frightened by hearing that she wishes to be introduced to *me*. If I *am* a wild beast, I cannot help it.

Ib., 24 May 1813

Poor Mrs C. Milles, that she should die on a wrong day at last, after being about it so long!

Ib., 13 March 1817

'I have lately taken it into my head to think (perhaps with little reason) that my complexion is by no means equal to the rest of my face and have therefore taken, as you see, to white and red paint, which I would scorn to use on any other occasion, as I hate art.'

(Rebecca), *Frederic and Elfrida*, 3

Sophia shrieked and fainted on the ground – I screamed and instantly ran mad – . We remained thus mutually deprived of our senses some minutes, and on regaining them were deprived of them again.

For an hour and a quarter did we continue in this unfortunate situation. *Love and Friendship*, 13

Trivial Pursuits

Sir John was a sportsman, Lady Middleton a mother. He hunted and shot, and she humoured her children; and these were their only resources. *Sense and Sensibility*, 1.7

A sportsman, though he esteems only those of his sex who are sportsmen likewise, is not often desirous of encouraging their taste by admitting them to a residence within his own manor. *Ib.*

'I am afraid,' replied Elinor, 'that the pleasantness of an employment does not always evince its propriety.'

Ib., I.13

She was a great wonderer, as every one must be who takes a very lively interest in all the comings and goings of all their acquaintance. *Ib.*, I.14

'We never could agree in our choice of a profession. I always preferred the church, as I still do. But that was not smart enough for my family. They recommended the army. That was a great deal too smart for me.'

(Edward Ferrars), *Ib.*, I.19

Edward had no turn for great men or barouches. All his wishes centered in domestic comfort and the quiet of private life. Fortunately he had a younger brother who was more promising. [Edward Ferrars]

Ib., I.3

'I was therefore entered at Oxford and have been properly idle ever since.'

(Edward Ferrars), *Ib.* I.19

'A man who has nothing to do with his own time has no conscience in his intrusion on that of others.'

(Marianne Dashwood), *Ib.*, II.9

'I consider music as a very innocent diversion, and perfectly compatible with the profession of a clergyman.'

(Mr Collins), *Pride and Prejudice* , I.18

'Men love to distinguish themselves, and in either of the other lines, distinction may be gained, but not in the church. A clergyman is nothing.'

(Mary Crawford), *Mansfield Park*, I.9

'A clergyman has nothing to do but to be slovenly and selfish – read the newspaper, watch the weather, and quarrel with his wife. His curate does all the work, and the business of his own life is to dine.'   *Ib.*, I.11

He came on the wings of disappointment, and with his head full of acting.   *Ib.*, I.13

Over the mantlepiece still hung a landscape in coloured silks of her performance, in proof of her having spent seven years at a great school in town to some effect.

Sense and Sensibility, II.4

A real old-fashioned Boarding-school, where a reasonable quantity of accomplishments were sold at a reasonable price, and where girls might be sent to be out of the way and scramble themselves into a little education, without any danger of coming back prodigies.

Emma, I.3

'I had no idea that the law had been so great a slavery.'

(Mr Elton), *Ib.*, I.13

'The [Post-office] Clerks grow expert from habit. – They must begin with some quickness of sight and hand, and exercise improves them. If you want any further explanation,' continued he, smiling, 'they are paid for it.'

(John Knightley), *Ib.*, II.16

She gloried in being a sailor's wife, but she must pay the tax of quick alarm for belonging to that profession which is, if possible, more distinguished in its domestic virtues than in its national importance.   *Persuasion*, II.12

'The lawyer plods, quite care-worn; the musician is up at all hours, and travelling in all weather; and even the clergyman –' she stopt a moment to consider what might do for the clergyman; – 'and even the clergyman, you know is obliged to go into infected rooms, and expose his health and looks to all the injury of a poisonous atmosphere.'

(Mrs Clay), *Ib.*, I.3

'Sailors work hard enough for their comforts.'

(Anne Elliot), *Ib.*

'To be mistress of French, Italian, German, Music, Singing, Drawing etc., will gain a woman some applause, but will not add one lover to her list.'

(Lady Susan Vernon), *Lady Susan*

Caste Marks

'You and I, Sir John,' said Mrs Jennings, 'should not stand upon such ceremony.'
    'Then you would be very ill-bred,' cried Mr Palmer.
    'My love, you contradict every body,' – said his wife with her usual laugh. 'Do you know that you are quite rude?'
    'I did not know I contradicted any body in calling your mother ill-bred.'

(Mr & Mrs Palmer), *Sense and Sensibility*, I.20

The Netherfield ladies would have had difficulty believing that a man who lived by trade and within view of his own warehouses, could have been so well bred and agreeable.
Pride and Prejudice, II.2

'Mr Darcy may perhaps have *heard* of such a place as Gracechurch Street, but he would hardly think a month's ablution enough to cleanse him from its impurities were he once to enter it.'
(Elizabeth Bennet), *Ib.*

'A man in distressed circumstances has not time for all those elegant decorums which other people may observe.'
(Elizabeth Bennet), *Ib.*, II.4

'Lady Catherine will not think the worse of you for being simply dressed. She likes to have the distinction of rank preserved.'
(Mr Collins), *Ib.*, II.6

Whenever any of the cottagers were disposed to be quarrelsome, discontented or too poor, she sallied forth into the village to settle their differences, silence their complaints, and scold them into harmony and plenty.
[Lady Catherine De Bourgh]
Ib., II.7

'A younger son, you know, must be inured to self-denial and dependence.'
  'In my opinion, the younger son of an Earl can know very little of either.'
(Colonel Fitzwilliam & Elizabeth Bennet), *Ib.*, II.10

'It spared me the concern which I might have felt in refusing you, had you behaved in a more gentleman-like manner.'
(Elizabeth Bennet), *Ib.*, II.11

'But perhaps he may be a little whimsical in his civilities,' replied her uncle. 'Your great men often are.'
(Mr Gardiner), *Ib.*, III.1

'Are the shades of Pemberley to be thus polluted?'
(Lady Catherine De Bourgh), *Ib.*, III.14

'He is a gentleman; I am a gentleman's daughter; so far we are equal.'
(Elizabeth Bennet), *Ib.*

'I begin to understand you all, except Miss Price,' said Miss Crawford, as she was walking with the Mr Bertrams. 'Pray, is she out, or is she not?'   *Mansfield Park*, I.5

'Be honest and poor, by all means – but I shall not envy you; I do not much think I shall even respect you. I have a much greater respect for those that are honest and rich.'
                                                    (Mary Crawford), *Ib.*, II.4

I believe, there is scarcely a young lady in the united kingdoms, who would not rather put up with the misfortune of being sought by a clever, agreeable man, than have him driven away by the vulgarity of her nearest relations.   *Ib.*, III.10

'The yeomanry are precisely the order of people with whom I feel I can have nothing to do. A degree or two lower, and a creditable appearance might interest me.'
                                           (Emma Woodhouse), *Emma*, I.4

'If we feel for the wretched, enough to do all we can for them, the rest is empty sympathy, only distressing to ourselves.'   (Emma Woodhouse), *Ib.*, I.10

There are people, who the more you do for them, the less they will do for themselves.   *Ib.*, I.11

'You are very fond of bending little minds; but where little minds belong to rich people in authority, I think they have a knack of swelling out, till they are quite as unmanageable as great ones.'   (Emma Woodhouse), *Ib.*, I.18

There, not to be vulgar, was distinction and merit.
[Highbury]   *Ib.*, II.11

What she was, must be uncertain; but *who* she was might be found out.   *Ib.*, II.4

'A bride, you know, my dear, is always the first in company, let the others be who they may.'
                                              (Mr Woodhouse), *Ib.*, II.14

'One has not great hopes from Birmingham. I always say there is something direful in the sound.'
                                                  (Mrs Elton), *Ib.*, II.18

General benevolence, but not general friendship, made a
man what he ought to be. *Ib.*, III.2

'The nature and the simplicity of gentlemen and ladies,
with their servants and furniture, I think is best observed
by meals within doors.' (Mr Knightley), *Ib.*, III.6

Isabella had connected herself unexceptionably. She had
given them neither men, nor names, nor places, that could
raise a blush. *Ib.*

She had a great idea that people who had extensive
grounds themselves cared very little for the extensive
grounds of any body else. *Ib.*, II.14

Delightful, charming, superior, first circles, spheres, lines,
ranks, every thing. *Ib.*, III.6

The stain of illegitimacy, unbleached by nobility or wealth,
would have been a stain indeed. *Ib.*, III.19

'She was your governess, I think?'
Emma was almost too much astonished to answer; but
Mrs Elton hardly waited for the affirmative before she went
on.
'Having understood as much, I was rather astonished to
find her so very lady-like! But she is really quite the
gentlewoman.' (Mrs Elton & Emma Woodhouse), *Ib.*, II.14

'A little upstart, vulgar being, with her Mr E., and her *caro
sposo*, and her resources, and all her airs of pert pretension
and under-bred finery. Actually to discover that Mr
Knightley is a gentleman! I doubt whether he will return
the compliment, and discover her to be a lady.'
(Emma Woodhouse), *Ib.*, II.14

Mary had merely connected herself with an old country
family of respectability and large fortune, and had
therefore *given* all the honour, and received none.
Persuasion, I.1

'A man is in greater danger in the navy of being insulted by
the rise of one whose father, his father might have
disdained to speak to.'
(Sir Walter Elliot), *Ib.*, I.3

'I thought you were speaking of some man of property: Mr Wentworth was nobody.'   *Ib.*

'One wonders how the names of many of our nobility become so common.'   *Ib.*

'I have let my house to Admiral Croft,' would sound extremely well; very much better than to any mere *Mr.* – a *Mr* (save perhaps, some half dozen in the nation,) always needs a note of explanation.   *Ib.*

The Musgroves, like their houses, were in a state of alteration, perhaps of improvement.   *Ib.*, I.5

Every little social commonwealth should dictate its own matters of discourse.   *Ib.*, I.6

The Dalrymples considered the relationship as closed.
                                                                        Ib., II.4

'My idea of good company, Mr Elliot, is the company of clever, well-informed people, who have a great deal of conversation; that is what I call good company.'
    'You are mistaken,' said he gently, 'that is not good company, that is the best. Good company requires only birth, education and manners, and with regard to education is not very nice.'   (Anne Elliot & Mr Elliot), *Ib.*

'Woman of that class [nurses] have great opportunities, and if they are intelligent may be well worth listening to.'
                                                        (Anne Elliot), *Ib.*, II.5

'A widow Mrs Smith, lodging in Westgate-buildings! – A poor widow, barely able to live, between thirty and forty – a mere Mrs Smith, an every day Mrs Smith, of all people and all names in the world, to be the chosen friend of Miss Anne Elliot, and to be preferred by her, to her own family connections among the nobility of England and Ireland! Mrs Smith, such a name!'
                                                        (Sir Walter Elliot), *Ib.*

The theatre or the rooms, where he was most likely to be, were not fashionable enough for the Elliots, whose evening amusements were solely in the elegant stupidity of private parties.   *Ib.*, II.7

Elizabeth had been long enough in Bath, to understand the importance of a man of such an air and appearance as his. The past was nothing. The present was that Captain Wentworth would move about well in her drawing-room.

Ib., II.10

The Miss Beauforts were soon satisfied with 'the circle in which they moved in Sanditon' to use a proper phrase, for every body must now 'move in a circle', – to the prevalence of which rotatory motion, is perhaps to be attributed the giddiness and false steps of many. *Sanditon*, II

A country surgeon (dont tell Mr C. Lyford) would not be introduced to men of their rank. And when Mr Portman is first brought in he would not be introduced as *the Honourable*. That distinction is never mentioned at such times. Letters, 10 August 1814

As I am myself partial to the roman catholic religion, it is with infinite regret that I am obliged to blame the behaviour of any member of it: yet truth being I think very excusable in an historian, I am necessitated to say that in this reign the roman catholics of England did not behave like gentlemen to the protestants. Their behaviour indeed to the Royal Family and both Houses of Parliament might justly be considered by them as very uncivil.

James the 1st, *The History of England*

Reading & Writing

'I have been used to consider poetry as the *food* of love,' said Darcy.

'Of a fine, stout, healthy love it may. Every thing nourishes what is strong already. But if it be only a slight thin sort of inclination, I am convinced that one good sonnet will starve it entirely away.'

(Elizabeth Bennet & Mr Darcy), *Pride and Prejudice*, I.9

Because they were fond of reading, she fancied them satirical. *Sense and Sensibility*, II.14

Let other pens dwell on guilt and misery. I quit such odious
subjects as soon as I can.   *Mansfield Park*, III.17

Let us leave it to the Reviewers to abuse such effusions of
fancy at their leisure, and over every new novel to talk in
threadbare strains of the trash with which the press now
groans.   *Northanger Abbey*, I.5

There seems almost a general wish of decrying the capacity
and undervaluing the labour of the novelist, and of
slighting the performances which have only genius, wit,
and taste to recommend them.   *Ib.*

'And what are you reading, Miss-?'
   'Oh! it is only a novel!'   *Ib.*

'It is only Cecilia, or Camilla, or Belinda;' or, in short, only
some work in which the greatest powers of the mind are
displayed, in which the most thorough knowledge of
human nature, the happiest delineation of its varieties, the
liveliest effusions of wit and humour are conveyed to the
world in the best chosen language.   *Ib.*

The substance of its papers so often consisting in the
statement of improbable circumstances, unnatural
characters, and topics of conversation, which no longer
concern any one living; and their language, too, frequently
so coarse as to give no very favourable idea of the age that
could endure it. [The *Spectator*]   *Ib.*

'The person, be it gentleman or lady, who has not pleasure
in a good novel, must be intolerably stupid.'
                                    (Henry Tilney), *Ib.*, I.14

'I am fond of history.'
   'I wish I were too. I read it a little as a duty, but it tells
me nothing that does not either vex or weary me. The
quarrels of popes and kings, with wars or pestilences, in
every page; the men all so good for nothing, and hardly any
women at all.'
                        (Miss Tilney & Catherine Morland), *Ib.*

'I have heard that something very shocking indeed, will
soon come out in London.'
                            (Catherine Morland), *Ib.*

Alas! if the heroine of one novel be not patronized by the
heroine of another, from whom can she expect protection
and regard?   *Ib.*, I.5

Sir Walter Elliot, of Kellynch-hall, in Somersetshire, was a
man who, for his own amusement, never took up any book
but the Baronetage; there he found occupation for an idle
hour, and consolation in a distressed one; there his faculties
were roused into admiration and respect.   *Persuasion*, I.1

The sweet scenes of autumn were for a while put by –
unless some tender sonnet, fraught with the apt analogy of
the declining year, with declining happiness, and the
images of youth and hope, and spring, all gone together,
blessed her memory.   *Ib.*, I.10

She ventured to hope he did not always read only poetry;
and to say, that she thought it was the misfortune of poetry,
to be seldom safely enjoyed by those who enjoyed it
completely; and that the strong feelings which alone could
estimate it truly, were the very feelings which ought to
taste it but sparingly.   *Ib.*, I.11

'You know what he thinks of Cowper and Scott; you are
certain of his estimating their beauties as he ought, and you
have received every assurance of his admiring Pope no
more than is proper.'

(Elinor Dashwood), *Sense and Sensibility*, I.10

They walked together some time, talking as before of Mr
Scott and Lord Byron, and still as unable, as before, and as
unable as any other two readers, to think exactly alike of
the merits of either.   *Persuasion*, I.12

'Shakespeare one gets acquainted with without knowing
how. It is part of an Englishman's constitution.'

(Henry Crawford), *Mansfield Park*, III.3

She would learn to be an enthusiast for Scott and Lord
Byron; nay, that was probably learnt already; of course they
had fallen in love over poetry.   *Persuasion*, II.6

'This,' said she, 'is nearly the sense, or rather the meaning
of the words, for certainly the sense of an Italian love-song
must not be talked of.'

(Anne Elliot), *Ib.*, II.8

'I really cannot be plaguing myself for ever with all the new poems and states of the nation that come out. Lady Russell quite bores one with her new publications.'

(Miss Elliot), *Ib.*, II.10

'Men have had every advantage of us in telling their own story. Education has been theirs in so much higher a degree; the pen has been in their hands.'

(Anne Elliot), *Ib.*, II.11

'I will not allow books to prove any thing.'

Ib.

It would be an affront to my readers were I to suppose they were not as well acquainted with the particulars of this king's reign as I am myself.

Henry the 8th, *The History of England*

I am never too busy to think of S&S. I can no more forget it, than a mother can forget her sucking child.

Letters, 25 April 1811

I think she will like my Elinor, but cannot build on anything else. [Elinor Dashwood, *Sense and Sensibility*]

Ib.

I want to tell you that I have got my own darling child from London. [*Pride and Prejudice*]

Ib., 29 January 1813

I must confess that I think her as delightful a creature as ever appeared in print, and how I shall be able to tolerate those who do not like *her* at least I do not know. [Elizabeth Bennet, *Pride and Prejudice*]

Ib.

I have scratched out Sir Tho. from walking with the other men to the stables etc. the very day after his breaking his arm – for though I find your papa *did* walk out immediately after *his* arm was set, I think it can be so little usual as to *appear* unnatural in a book.

Ib., 10 August 1814

We think you had better not leave England. Let the Portmans go to Ireland, but as you know nothing of the manners there, you had better not go with them. You will be in danger of giving false representation.

Ib.

3 or 4 Families in a country village is the very thing to work on.

Ib., 9 September 1814

To those readers who have prefered 'Pride and Prejudice' it will appear inferior in wit, and to those who have preferred 'Mansfield Park' very inferior in good sense. [*Emma*]

Ib., 11 December 1815

I think I may boast myself to be, with all possible vanity, the most unlearned and uninformed female who ever dared to be an authoress.

Ib.

The little bit (two inches wide) of ivory on which I work with so fine a brush, as produces little effect after much labour.

Ib., 16 December 1816